Examining

The Root

of

All EVIL

By

Bill McBride

An American Social Critic

About the Author

Bill McBride lives in San Jose, California. A Leo, he was born in early August of 1950 in a slightly mountainous area of the Northwestern Arkansas Ozarks. McBride attended public school at Pea Ridge, Arkansas and received his High School Diploma in May of 1968. He began college in June that year at the age of 17 at Branson, Missouri at the College of the School of the Ozarks. However in March of 1969 he dropped out for six months due to depression. In July of 1969, William E. McBride became a Newspaper Reporter for the Miami News-Record in the rural town of Miami, Oklahoma.

Between June of 2002 and October 4, 2003, Bill McBride lived in all four major USA Time Zones. He moved from Albuquerque to Farmington, New Mexico to Tacoma, Washington, to Des Moines, Iowa to Orlando Florida to Monterrey, California. In June of 2009 he moved from Salinas, California to San Jose, California where he presently lives near downtown.

McBride has been interested in writing since 1963. His book, "Examining The Root of All Evil," explores and exposes over 250 examples of EVIL, and what some people have labeled as Evil. There are no chapters in this book, because the various forms of Evil are presented in Alphabetical Order. All letters from A to Z are represented. But he is sure there have been very few Evil Zebras, but an Xacto knife probably could kill someone.

In 1986, William McBride received his BA in Psychology at a wonderful smalltown university, New Mexico Highlands University at Las Vegas, New Mexico, USA. His last job as a journalist was with the Clovis News-Journal during the Summer of 1987. On August 12th, 1987, Bill had his last drink. He's been sober ever since, and marks August 14, 1987 as his Sobriety Birthdate. He hopes to have a second book out before the start of

Spring of 2024 designed for blatant "Know-It-All's" in an effort to help them to have Sweeter Personalities.

Foreword

Hello my name is William Eugene McBride, mostly known as Bill McBride.   Mine is not a real common name like many Hispanic and Anglo-Saxon Last Names. Yet, there are many Bill McBride's on Social Media as well as in real life.

Over the years, I've been placed in many boxes.   Some of those nasty, smelly boxes I got placed in by other people or by institutions.   Most of us Human Beings disdain being placed in a box or being labeled. Yet, this is a Universal Human Failing. We do to others what we definitely do not want them doing to us.

But, never-the-less our language orientation and our school, society at large, our worship centers and our family or origin all contribute to us becoming a sluggard or a genius -- or just a hard-working law-abiding citizen of the world.   And what's wrong with being a hard-working law-abiding citizen?

Lisping boys, girls who hate Barbie Dolls, and anyone who just doesn't fit in to the so-called normal soon get labeled at Deviant. If not by their Parents and Siblings, then by School, Church, or the Police.

One of my Agnostic Friends was labeled at a very young age by a Nun at his elementary school as a Problem Child. Because he had early signs of being Gay, the teacher thought that he was Demon Possessed.

In fact, one extreme evil we have here in the Dis-United States is the way we "Demonize" politicians, religious leaders, doctors, presidents and almost anyone from the West Coast. Many years ago I was told I was demon-possessed by a fellow student at a Catholic-oriented university.

I have a theory about Demon Possession. During the time 2000+ years ago that Jesus of Nazareth walked the roads and streets of

Israel he met many demon possessed people, whom he quickly healed. He didn't flash a cross or a million dollar smile. Possession is serious stuff. I believe that Jesus of Nazareth, my Savior, more often known as Jesus Christ, healed dozens, maybe hundreds or more of their spirit being overruled by a powerful mind and body controlling demon spirit. Folks, we've been living in the Last Days since the Day of Pentecost (Acts -- Chapter 2).

However, in the last 150 years the doctrine of a Pre-Tribulation Rapture has evolved and much of Christianity embraces this doctrine. So there are a number of Theories about the Rapture of the Church, of the End of the Age, the Tribulation, the Reign of the Anti-Christ, and the Second Coming of Christ, God's Holy Angels, Wicked Angels, Satan (Lucifer or the Devil) and Demonology and Demon Spirits. When the theory of the Rapture is opened-up, it seems that Jesus will return two more times before the final judgment.

"Where are you getting two more times from," you may be saying. Well, Jesus doesn't touch his feet to the Earth when he returns the second time, as in the Pre-Tribulation Rapture. However, when he returns after the peaceful, perfect solutions Christ-like Impostor has reigned for at a minimum of seven years -- this third arrival to planet Earth -- Jesus the Christ will not be an Innocent Baby in a Manager. He comes back as Judge of the Universe and his first target will be the Impostor Anti-Christ. Will that person be a man or woman, or perhaps a Trans Person who can switch back and forth in their clothing appearance? Is this person already alive? Today most of us people in the USA believe we are living in the true Last Days.

I too believe in the Last Days. And according to the Demonology Theory by Bill McBride (first published right here) Demon Possession is everywhere. So is the popularity of White Magic, Atheism, Demonic Worship, Satanic Worship, Agnosticism, Narcissism, and etc. The Shadowy effect of Darkness abounds in places around the world. New Age teachers insist that everybody is GOOD, that Evil is Live spelled backwards. And both the Good and the UN-Good come to us from the Universe (which includes not only the Creator but all aspects of the Supernatural.) Don't they realize that the Supernatural also includes the works and miracles done by our enemy, Satan, and his thousands of evil fallen angels.

So, let's review. Demons are Real; God is Real; the Devil (the creator of Evil) is Real; Covid-19 is Real; America is the Great Satan -- well that's probably Real too.

Here in the United States demon possessed people walk and talk among us. So does Bank Presidents, Politicians, Preachers, School Teachers, myself, yourself, and thousands of House-less People. Just because someone appears to be talking to themselves doesn't make them crazy, stupid, or demon-possessed. Oh my, I'm putting people into crazy, tiny, smelly boxes myself. I have often asserted that I'm a Non-Judgmental Person. "Bill McBride, welcome to the Real World!"

In my research on examples of Evil that now exist here in the second decade of the 21st Century -- it appears that Human Evil pervades our society and our Planet. All may be sinful, but none of us were created Evil. It's an acquired taste.

As the Rev. Donnie Swaggart said on a telecast on SBN (Son-Life Broadcasting Network back in May of 2021, "Evil is an Equal Opportunity Destroyer." Evangelist Donnie Swaggart, the son of the Rev. Jimmy Swaggart and Sister Francis Swaggart of Baton Rouge, Louisiana.

Evangelist Joyce Meyer, another Pentecostal-style minister and well-known Christian motivational speaker has this to say about Evil. "Never blame GOD for the Evil and Wickedness in the world!"   --- Joyce Meyer (Ministries) of Felton, Missouri

My book reveals Blatant and Subconscious Evil in over 250 different forms.   I'm looking at Society, Politics, Religion,

Governments, Families, Employers, and the Tribe known as Human Beings. I know there is EVIL in my Heart from time to time. Perhaps there's just a little bitty, tiny bit of EVIL in your life also.

I have no desire to condemn everyone to Hell. There's way too much of that in our world today. I say these people practice what I call the "Hell-Destination Assignment Syndrome." Some of these people consign people to Hell on a regular basis. These are the "Hell and Brimstone" preachers and thousands of their followers. How seldom do we see a stranger ask another, "Are you Heaven Bound?" Sounds a bit less offensive than, "If you died tonight, do you have assurance in your heart that you would be going to Heaven and not to Hell?"

So, I, Bill McBride, challenge you as you read this book to keep an open mind and laugh anytime you want to say, "Hey McBride, what were you smoking when you figured out that situation as being Evil?" For the record I've been Sober since August 14, 1987 (Clovis, New Mexico) and Substance-Free since Feb. 16, 2003 (Des Moines, Iowa). While I'm a terrible Sponsor and Sponsee, both God and the Twelve Step programs helped me to break free. I've had many excellent sponsors in Alcoholics Anonymous, and a few who took me out for dinner and we never talked again.

The Disclaimer

Now the Disclaimer: I am not a medical person.   I am not a preacher (but you'll probably think differently as you read my various books). And, I'm not a Comedian. Well actually I am. I Suck at that almost as bad as I do at being a Waiter.

Somehow, I have never had an opulent lifestyle. Through the love and grace of God -- plus getting help from Social Services in many states -- I have survived.   I have a fairly healthy Self-Esteem and I've been able to avoid the Suicide Ward when I went into a mental health hospitals for being burned-out and overly-stressed.   My first trip was at age 18 when I was a college student and was about 100 to 150 miles away from home for the first time.

Read this book for Edification, for Enjoyment, for Humor, and for something to do to engage your mind when you are sitting on the bathroom throne.   This is my first published book.   There have been other attempts, but they got washed away by the Tide. I'm striving and will be happy to have this book as a "Bathroom Reader." Sure, most new authors want their work to be a "Coffee Table Book".   Dar-lyn, this ain't one of those 'high flu tin' books.

Enjoy and impress your friends with your new knowledge of the Evilness of Evil as you leisurely read, *The Root of all EVIL..* I have placed Evil not in categories or chapters, but in segments of the Alphabet.   And from time to time, I'll attempt to present both sides of an issue with quotations. And my personal opinion and experience is occasionally mentioned.

With over 250 examples of purported EVIL mentioned in my book, it was extremely hard to choose a suitable title that was inclusive as well as interesting and thought provoking. I almost settled on *"Blank Space Is the Root of all EVIL."* Eventually I settled on the present title, despite the fact that there are a number of books by various authors which all have the same title. Ironically, a non-relative, the Rev. Bill McBride previously published a book also on evil, also titled, "The Root of all Evil." I hope to read it soon, and I hope my book spurs more sales of his book in the religious community.

Bill McBride -- Writer-Artist since 1965 – Addictions Speaker – Motivational Speaker.

Japantown Neighborhood — Downtown -- San Jose, CA. USA 95112

August 29, 2021 – Published by BookTrail Agency - Publishers of Kansas City, MO.

The Root of All Evil

A-A-A-A-A

Abortion Clinics

Abortion on Demand

Apathy

Attitude

Nasty Attitude

Self-Righteous Attitude

Superior Attitude

Not Good Enough Attitude

Lack of Appreciation

AMERICA

Absurdity

Anxiety

Atheism

ANTIFA (The Group ANTIFA)

Agnostics

B-B-B-B-B

Betting

Banks

Bankers

Begging

Being - (Being a "Know It All")

Broken Promises

Broadway

Broadway Entertainment

Broadway Shows

BLM – (Black Lives Matter)

Bewitched – (Bewitched" The sitcom TV Show from the Fifties and Sixties.   Samantha and Darrin. He's Mortal and she is a Witch. But the real witch is His mother-in-law, Endora. Oops! Was that a Sexist Comment?)

Bacteria

C-C-C-C-C

Covid-19 - (The Virus which infected the whole world in 2020.)

Climate Change ---- Formerly known as Global Warming. Believed to have been caused by Green House Gases building up in Earth's Atmosphere. This toxic buildup is being and has been created because of pollution caused by Carbon Dioxide emissions from gasoline powered automobiles and coal burning sources. Most of the coal burning air pollutants come from home   furnaces and electrical generating power plants. Since the Three Mile Island Nuclear Power Plant Episode of the Winter of 1976 near Harrisburg, PA., there are very few locations where electrical power comes from Nuclear Energy.

Global Warming (Green House Gases) have affected our entire world atmosphere. Some places have suffered more than others. There is a tear in the ozone layer above Australia, according to Scientists. And both Antarctica and the Arctic regions of the planet have experienced major overheating which has resulted in iceberg break-offs, ice mountains falling into the oceans, and loss of habitat for Penguins and Polar Bears.

Global Warming is almost as divisive as Racism in causing the war between the Politicians and the Conservative Christians. I assert that Democrats Believe that "Republicans Deny and loudly assert that Democrats Deceive." Both sides can't be right. Yet, both sides are responsible for the political and social split that plagues the United States of America in the second decade of the 21st Century.

Child Abuse

Child Abuse --- This may be an idea that you have never considered, but I ask you to indulge me for the next three minutes. I believe the first humans to be guilty of Child Abuse were Adam and Eve. "Preposterous," you say. This is not brought out in the Bible, but a few verses after Adam and Eve are removed from the Garden of Eden we're hearing about God rejecting the offering of Vegetables and Fruits offered to Him by their first child, Cain.

In fact as the fifth child in a family of eight children, I assert that I was an abused child, because I was an invisible child. I was very busy but I was always vying for any form of acceptance and recognition. What I didn't realize then was that Life Is Often Hard for People and my Parents were very busy with being Parents. I was the bratty kid who asked too many hard questions, who wanted to be included in all the games and who never had any help with my schoolwork.

In Genesis 4 - We aren't told how old Cain and Abel were at this time, but they were at least teenagers, and most likely over age 18. Abel's offering pleased God because it was a spotless animal free of any blemish. But the world's first successful gardener, Cain, offered the best of his garden to the Lord, but this act didn't please God, because Cain had not followed instructions.

I assert that Adam and Eve had spent much of their life ignoring Cain. Fruits and Vegetables responded to this touch and his attention. If Mom and Dad didn't show him enough attention, at least he could be proud of the excellent beautiful produce of his garden. This productive garden grew on the ground of a planet that had been cursed by God Himself for the sin of Cain's parents because they had eaten of the forbidden fruit back a few years earlier when they had lived in the beautiful, indescribable Garden of Eden. Genesis 4:1-13.

Had Adam and Eve ever told their children about the wrath of God? And what about their sin back in the bountiful beautiful

Garden of Eden and the terrible consequences of disobedience or the acts of giving in to the temptations of Sin?   I doubt it.

Most likely Adam and Eve's second child, Abel, the shepherd, was born fairly soon after the birth of Cain.   I believe that Cain's Child Abuse was the act of being ignored. Mom and Dad devoted their attention to the second child because Abel was the Baby and Babies need more attention.

I was born in early August of 1950 but in only a little over 16 months my sister was born in mid-January of 1952. I believe that a well- adjusted child becomes a well-adjusted adult. Because some of us don't have enough time being "The Baby", we grow up feeling lonely, secluded, invisible and unloved. Great Mentors, Caring Therapists a Loving God and an attitude of Forgiveness finally helped me to forgive and accept my childhood upbringing.

Adam and Eve had to make a living from a tough hostile environment and then cute little Abel showed up. No wonder Cain turned out like he did. Then having his treasured offering rejected by the God of the Universe was the Last Straw. Abel was Mom and Dad's favorite and obviously he was also God's favorite too.   Who needed His Sweet Perfect Brother anyway.   He certainly didn't and the next tinc they quarreled he pounded his brother on the head with a boulder from the garden. And He realized after the Murder that "We are indeed 'Our Brother's Keeper;'" and shortly thereafter Cain's nightmare began.

Confusication --- Something so confusing or complicated that it's difficult to explain. The Urban Dictionary says: "The particular combination of Consternation and Confusion produced when one asks a painful or awkward question that nobody wants to answer.   [And the questioner responds] 'I'm sorry for the Confusication caused by my question, I don't mean to offend.

Condemnation

Clarity -- Refusing to Ask Clarifying questions

Confusion

Corporations

(Big Corporations)

(Monopolistic Corporations)

Conservative People

Conservative Religious People (Usually expressed by Democrats and Liberal Thinkers)

Cults

"Charmed" -- the TV Show about three female relatives who are witches.   The good kind.

D-D-D-D-D

Discontent

Democrats

Damnation

The Devil

Disappointment

Demonizing Someone

Deception

Disobedience

E-E-E-E-E

Everything -- There's somebody who is going to label something innocent, no matter how innocent, as being Evil.   However, if Mom and Dad call it Evil, we better pay attention.

Empathy

European Union also known as the European Community.

The Euro

Excuses:

Two of the biggest ones are:

"I'm sorry, but that's not part of my Job Description."

"Sorry, I'm Too Busy to Hear What You Want To Tell Me."

Easy -- "Oh He / She -- is too Easy."   I'm sure you've heard someone say this about another person who is sexually active, but unmarried or committing adultery.

F-F-F-F-F

Fake -- Fake News

The "F" Word. It's not in the Bible. It wasn't used by Shakespeare. Charles Dickens never had it spoken by any of his many characters. It is believed to have evolved in Germany, less than 400 years ago....and daily it offends thousands of believers.

Failure To Act

Failure

Failure sometimes results in Bad Things Happening, but most Successful People and most Motivational Leaders believe that Failure helps us move forward. Unfortunately millions of people give up when they have a string of failures. Thomas Edison failed to invent the light bulb thousands of times before he found the correct substance that wouldn't instantly burn up when he turned on the electricity. My advice is Be Careful, but Embrace Failure. God has used thousands of people who others considered failures to further His Work on our Planet Earth.

The gods

GOD

GOD -- The Concept that there is only One God.

GOD -- The Concept of the Trinity.   God has three personalities -- God the Father; God the Son (Jesus Christ); and God the Holy Spirit.

GOD --   Atheism teaches that Humanity created the concept of Religion and the need for having a Higher Power to enhance your Life.

Gossip

Garden of Eden

Greenhouse Gases -- Automobile emissions and smoke from chimneys cause Carbon Monoxide and Carbon Dioxide to be expelled into Earth's Atmosphere.   This affects the clouds and the atmosphere many miles high above our planet. Creating a situation which blocks the good rays of the Sun.   Carbon Dioxide in small amounts is taken-in by trees and other plants and is beneficial to the plant -- such as breathing oxygen is beneficial to us humans and to other mammals.

Quote:

"The big damages come if Climate Sensitivity to greenhouse gases turn out to be high causing greater global warming than current projections. Then it's not a bullet headed at us, but a thermonuclear warhead.

Raymond Pierrehumbert -- PICTUREQUOTES.COM

Game Playing

Some of the Games People Play:

* "Name Game"

* "Blame Game"

* "Bullying Game"

* "Victim Game"

* "Vindicator Game"

* "Rescuer"

* "Parental Game"

* "Child's Game"

Gnosticism

Global Warming --- Discussed already under "Climate Change".

Germs

H-H-H-H-H

Hollywood

Hate

Hatred

Haters

Homophobia

Homophobia Quotes:

"It's not loving a man that makes life harder for gay guys. It's homophobia. It's not the color of their skin that makes life harder for people of color; it's racism. It's not having vaginas that makes life harder for women, it's sexism. - And its ageism, far more than the passage of time, that makes gowing old harder for us all."

--- Ashton Applewhite,

This Chair Rocks: A Manifesto Against Ageism

"What's unnatural is homophobia. Homo sapiens is the only species in all of nature that responds with hate to homosexuality."

--- Alex Sanchez, The God Box

Homeless People

Homelessness

Homelessness Quotations:

"The poverty of being unwanted, unloved, and uncared for is the greatest poverty. We must start in our homes to remedy this kind of poverty."

-- Mother Teresa

"Most people never really sat down and got to know a homeless person but every homeless person is just a real person that was created by God and is the same kind of different as us; they just have a different story."

-- Ron Hall

Our Father's House Soup Kitchen

Pompano Beach, FL. - USA

Human Needs Ignored

Helpfulness --- Some people feel you can be too helpful. This is how they define one "Being too Helpful. -- "Don't give to the Homeless, they'll just spend the money on Liquor or Drugs."

Hopelessness

Helplessness

Homosexuality

Homosexuality Quotations:

"Love is a Human Experience -- not a Political Statement."

-- Anne Hathaway, Actress

"I think the best day will be when we no longer talk about being gay or straight. It's not a gay wedding, it's just a wedding....It's not a gay marriage, it's just a marriage. –

PINK, 21st Century Singer

"The Lord is my Shepherd and he knows I'm gay."

Troy Perry

A former Pentecostal Minister came-out to his wife as a gay man in the late sixties.   Within a few hours he had to appear before the church

leadership because his wife told them what he had confessed. Soon he was unemployed, and without a family or his church. The Rev. Troy Perry founded the Metropolitan Community Church, a world-wide Christian demonimation whose main outreach is to the LGBTQ community.

M.C.C. A church "that welcomes everyone" was founded in Los Angeles in 1969 by Troy Perry and 12 gay men and his supportive mother.

His book "The Lord Is My Shepherd and He Knows I'm Gay" has helped thousands of men and women decide that they can be both Gay and Christian. Not all Christians agree, however.

Harry Potter

Not Having.....

*Not Having a Facebook Account.

* Not Having an Email Address.

* Not Having a Twitter Account.

* Not Having a Mission Statement to guide your Life.

* Not Having a Good Sense of Humor.

* Not Having a Relationship.

* Not Having a Spouse.

And there is also having; such as Having a....

* Having a Sense of Impending Doom.

* Having a Wicked Sense of Humor.

* Having a Co-Dependent Friend of Relative.

* Having a Facebook Account.

* Having a Twitter Account.

* Having an Email Account.

I-I-I-I-I

Ignoring Other People

Ignoring the Awful Pain of Another Person or an Animal that hurts.

Ideals

"Ignoring the Elephant in the Room."

I

I -- as in "Me":

I - "Is it I Lord?   Am I EVIL?"

"I believe if we all said, 'I am one of the roots of all evil,' and then asked God to take that away from us, the world could become a much Better and Safer place. Because if Christianity is correct, and I believe it is, all humans are evil. The Bible establishes that early on in the book of Genesis. The book of the Psalms and the book Proverbs declare how to be good and the works of evil. Among the hundreds of Proverbs there are many references to Evil. Evil can be found in every person in hundreds of situations and is immortalized in our Planet's History

MY QUOTE: "I believe if we all said, 'I am one of the roots of all evil,' and then asked God to take that away from us, the world could become a much Better and

Safer place. Because if Christianity is correct -- and I believe it is -- all humans are Evil."

 --- Bill McBride, Author -- "The Root of All Evil."

Inspiration -- Your desire to improve yourself, your family, your environment, or society as a whole. It's not fair, but there will always be people who will look you in the eye, as they look down their nose and icily say to you, "Just who do you think you are!" Meaning....you're getting "Too Big for your Britches" (your Pants); or "You're not qualified."

Ignoring the Obvious

Irresponsible Decision Making

Ignoring Others

Inattention

Irresponsibility

Illuminati

Inability

Inability to Ask Relevant Questions

One's Inability to ASK Questions influences many things. Let me break it down:

* The Inability to Ask Sufficient Red Flag Questions; Seek Answers from Your High Power; then make a Timely Decision and then move forward to complete the task -- this psychological disability which I myself and many other people possess -- could that be a Root of All Evil?"

"I'm too Busy to Listen to What You are Trying to Tell Me."

Indolent

Indulgent

J-J-J-J-J

Judgmental

Joking Around

Jerk

Being a Jerk.   Some people would say this person should not be called a

"Jerk" but a seven-letter word that starts with an "A".

K-K-K-K-K

The KKK

Known as the Klu Klux Klan -- Active after the Civil War when racist White Men would place a white bed sheet over their heads and terrorize Black Families and Black Residents of their local area. Still in existence in 21st century America.

Know -- "The Know-It-All", the not-so-popular family member or friend who knows the solution to everyone else's problems. And they make sure everyone knows how wise they are, and that they are ready to share.

L-L-L-L-L

Laziness

Lying

Legalism

Liberalism

Lack

Lack -- Life has many Lacks.   So, let's look at some lacks that other people or yourself may perceive as Evil:

* Lack of Sufficient Education

* Lack of Money

* Lack of a Mate

* Lack of a Spouse

* Lack of a Date

* Lack of Authority

* Lack of Positive Self Talk

* Lack of Sleep

* Lack of Cash

* Lack of a Bank Account

* Lack of Housing

* Lack of Joy

* Lack of Happiness

* Lack resulting because your Basic Human Needs are not being satisfied. (This is one evil which permeates much of the world.)

* Lack of Appreciation

* Lack of Recognition

* Lack of Empathy

* Lack of Encouragement

* Lack of Good Morals

* Lack of Interest

Next let's look at some situations where something once unlawful has now been legalized (especially here in the USA).

The Legalization of:

* Abortion

* Abortion Rights

* Gay Rights

* Transgender Rights

* Gay and Lesbian Marriages

* Marijuana Use

M-M-M-M-M

* Money is the Root of All Evil

* Making Impossible Promises

* Making False Promises

* Mission Statement -- Not having one to inspire and guide your life.

* Monarchies

* Matrimony

* Monogamy

* Monopolies

* Monotheistic Theology

N-N-N-N-N

New Age

The Teachings of New Ages Teachers

New World Order

Nazi Germany and the Holocaust

Nazism

Not

Not -- Evil involving the word - NOT:

* Not taking Action.

* Not Paying Attention.

* Not Having Your Basic Needs Supplied.

* Not Accepting the Obvious Truth.

* Not Accepting the Obvious Truth about the 2020 Election.

O-O-O-O-O

Obscenities

Opinion

Offensive Opinion

Being Obstinate

P-P-P-P-P

Passing the Buck

The Papacy

The Pope

Politics

Porn

Profanity

Propaganda

Procrastination

Pain

Expecting a Pain-Free Life.   As Doctor Phil says, "How's that working for you?"

Prejudice

Pagans

Paganism

The Powerful 2 %

Public Shaming

Plagues

Pestilence

Pandemics -- For Example the way many governments handled the Covid-19 Pandemic. Most leaders didn't have the heart to put restrictions in place early, especially the wearing of masks.

Q-Q-Q-Q-Q

Quiet Time

Queens

Queers

R-R-R-R-R

Racial Inequality

Religion

Riches

Relatives

Republicans

Rich People

Regret

The Rapture

Rapture Haters

The Pre-Tribulation Rapture

44

Refusing to Ask Clarifying Questions

Refusing to Follow Instructions

S-S-S-S-S

Slander -- Telling Lies about someone else.

Suicide

Socialism

Science

Social Sciences

Science Fiction

Sense of Humor

Sin

Sinners

Stupidity

Self-Discovery

Self-Esteem

Self-Improvement

Self-Improvement. Can it really be bad?   Some religious groups believe that psychological improvement is Sinful. They call it using Humanistic Psychology, and that Sigmund Freud and his followers practice Evil, by helping to heal the mind without prayer and Jesus being involved.

There is one form of Self Improvement which seems to be okay. That's Improving your home environment thanks to the hardware stores and the "DIY" (Do It Yourself) movement.

Sadism

Slavery

Selective Hearing

Selfishness

Sin -- Adam and Eve and Original Sin.   See the first few books of Genesis in God's Holy Bible.

Satan

The Great Satan -- Islam's label to describe America.

Superiority

Sharing

Sharing -- Actually "Not Sharing" -- When someone knows an answer to a known problem but will not share an Answer or Solution to a Critical Situation or Event because they have peculiar reasons for not doing so.

Screaming Obscene Words

Screaming Obscene Words is what everyone else does when someone realizes that the person with the Solution didn't reveal it.

T-T-T-T-T

Two-Timing --   When one's date, partner, or Fiancée is dating another person or more than one other person.

Thorns -- hen Christ went to the Cross; someone placed a Crown of Thorns on His head before he was nailed to the Cross.

Thorns -- Thorns were part of the curse that God placed upon the ground of Planet Earth after expelling Adam and Eve from the plentiful

Garden of Eden.   Genesis Chapter 3.

Thirst -- Happens to Humans and all Mammals.   Many of us have the mistaken belief that we can replace our need for Water with colas and energy drinks.   The bad news is that we can't.

Transgender -- "Denoting or relating to a person whose sense of personal identity and gender does not correspond with their birth sex." -- unknown dictionary.

The CDC in Atlanta says: "'Transgender' is an umbrella term for persons whose gender identity or expression (masculine, feminine, other) is different from their sex (male, females) at birth. 'Gender Identity' refers to one's own gender, or the gender with which a person identifies. 'Gender expression' is a term used

to describe people's outward presentation of their gender.'
www.CDC.gov (Transgender Persons).

Transgender Sexuality

Trans People are looked down upon by Straights, Gays, and
Homophobic Christians.   But not by everyone.

U-U-U-U-U

Unbelief in a Higher Power

Unbelief in God

Unbelief in Jesus Christ

Unacceptable Situations. When someone feels:

* Unappreciated.

* Unrecognized.

* Unrewarded.

* Unwelcomed.

Unfriend -- A term created because of social media. To be Unfriended on Facebook occurs when another user decides to declare that you are no longer their Friend.

Utopia -- The Humanistic Need to Have a Perfect Society and Environment.   Since Adam and Eve were banned from the Garden or Eden, people have been trying to create a Utopia on Earth.   It will happen during the 1,000-year Millennium when Jesus rules a perfectly re-perfected world from the city of Jerusalem.

While we don't live in a perfect world, I do believe God wants us to strive to better our World.

V-V-V-V-V

Vocabulary

Having a good Vocabulary is one sign of a well-rounded, well-educated person.   A Vocabulary without Profanity and Racial or Religious Slurs is desirable in the Christian world.

The Vatican

Vatican City -- Located in Rome, Italy.   Headquarters for the Roman Catholic Church, and the place where the Pope lives and from which he rules and reigns.

Victim-hood

W-W-W-W-W

War (Not listed in Original Book)

Wicca

Witchcraft

Witches and Warlocks

Working Women

Women's Lib

Wise Asses

Words

Worthwhileness

Worthlessness

54

Work

X-X-X-X-X
55

Xtra

Xacto Knife --- A cutting knife used by artists and mostly used for cutting paper.   Has replaceable blades.

Xenophobia -- See Zeno-phobia in the Z section.

Y-Y-Y-Y-Y

Yes Men

Yankees -- Not the Ball Team. In some parts of the American South, the word "Yankee" denotes one of those awful people from the North. A good friend from Naples, Florida once told me that anyone North of Tampa and Orlando was referred to as a Yankee. And even though I was a native of Arkansas, that made me a Yankee.

Z-Z-Z-Z-Z

Zeal

Zealous

Zealousness

Zealousness -- According to Bible Teachers the conversion of Saul of Tarsus resulted from his Jewish Zealousness. A well-educated young man, Saul had so much hatred for the followers of Jesus that he went to the Jewish Authorities at the Temple to get permission to arrest these New Testament Believers. On a trip from Jerusalem to Damascus, Saul had a spiritual and physically painful encounter with the Lord, Jesus Christ. Acts - Chapter 9. A few days later Saul became a Christian and after training with a few other believers that lasted for several years (perhaps as many as ten years) he gradually became trusted by the leaders of the Jerusalem Church. But before he became a Believer, Saul believed he was doing God's work by assisting in the Killing of Christians. He held the coats of the people who stoned Stephen the Deacon (Acts 6:8); who was accused of blasphemy after his heavy-hitting sermon about Moses. Saul's change from a hateful persecutor of the church to the Apostle Paul, who founded and taught many congregations around the Mediterranean Ocean, is given in the Back-Story in Acts 6 to 9. Acts 6:8 to Acts 9:19

Another Definition of Zealous.

Zealous One who is extremely enthusiastic. Such a person is often criticized by relatives, co-workers or associates.

Zen

Zebras

Zeno-phobia -- "Dislike of or prejudice against people from other countries."

Prologue

Thank you for reading my first published book. I hope you have enjoyed yourself and that you recognize Evil comes in many forms.

If you wish to draw nearer to the God of the Bible, I hope you will meet with a minister, priest, rabbi or holy dedicated person and will become a believer. May God be with you and Bless you on your Journey.

--- Bill McBride, Author.

Reviews Sections

www.ingramcontent.com/pod-product-compliance
Lightning Source LLC
Chambersburg PA
CBHW040111150726
48005CB00013B/1658